NAVIGATION

KATE CARRUTHERS THOMAS

INDEPENDENT INNOVATIVE INTERNATIONAL

Published by Cinnamon Press
Meirion House
Tanygrisiau
Blaenau Ffestiniog
Gwynedd, LL41 3SU
www.cinnamonpress.com

ISBN: 978-1-78864-021-3

British Library Cataloguing in Publication Data. A CIP record for this book can be obtained from the British Library.

Designed and typeset in Palatino by Cinnamon Press. Printed in Poland.

Cover design by Adam Craig

Cinnamon Press is represented in the UK by Inpress Ltd and in Wales by the Welsh Books Council.

Acknowledgements

I am indebted to Jan Fortune for her belief in my work and her careful mentorship and to her dedicated small team at Cinnamon Press for bringing this collection into being.

Contents

To Joyce Gibson Thomas (née Carruthers),
my mother,
who loves the colour turquoise
and who taught me to love language.

Navigation

After a drought

You speak to me in tongues. I need you to repeat
your strange vocabulary of desire. Tongue-tied
I try to find a voice.

You lie close. How did I survive without
another skin to trace, to taste; without
another heart transfusing mine?

You give your full attention. Frantic in its beam
I weep, consumed by grief for wasted time.

Now, I reply.

Navigation

We're climbing to Back Tor. Midsummer, but the black-brown peat
is sodden underfoot, unsteady. The light's behind us.
Clouds grey-swatched and speeding cancel out the view ahead.
Your eyes are on the map, converting three to two dimensions
as white-tipped drops hit plastic at forty-five degrees,
translating rising ground to contour, an ochre smear of water
as the ford. It's proof we're where we are.

I'm moving on towards the Tor, gritstone slabbed and glossy,
geology upturned. I scramble to the trig, a ship afloat
the oozing channels of the moor. I've got a bird's eye view of racing skies,
Whin Hill, the Coach and Horses ghostly on the western ridge.
Down below you measure out the millimetres, count paces forward,
thumb navigator's beads as if in prayer. We're where we are.
I long to take you on the glittering path across the moor to Lost Lad,

lose our bearings, risk the rain and kiss you.

Moving in

At noon I cross the threshold. You didn't know
essentials took up so much room
you say. You welcome me

with a passionate embrace. We consider
getting naked, drink tea, eat cake
instead. You haven't had the time you say

to clear a space for me. Forgive me?
I forgive. And so begins
a series of incursions: my pillow lurks

on your bed, my yellow bowls
like earthen suns nudge Royal Doulton,
my shoes trip over yours. Carefully

I insert myself into your life, adopt
corners as my own. Skirmishes occur.
Tea towels here or there?

A photograph I now know
to be precious, moved aside. We rage
and blow and go to bed. Lie

in each other's arms, invite each other in.
We're skin to skin. Each kiss
a homecoming.

Proposal

When I asked, you answered: Why?
You're right, who needs a seal
if life is like this sky, continually in motion
nephrology writ large?

At cruising altitude we watch
gulls brave choppy currents
testing strength and stretch,
turning white bellies to the sun.

Ravenglass

This year, returning to our blue-green portion
we inhale familiars: swifts netting air,
herons' shadow puppetry, low tide, all glass.
We sleep late, rediscover our capacity
to exhale, witness early evening estuary
swallow sky. At Drigg we walk together
between the river and the sea on salted, sand-stretched
land, marram-sprung, while westwards,
slate waves churn mud, retreat, but then like us
plan their return.

Tide

Poised on sandspit carved by water's slow suck,
a heron waits for prey.

Leans close, then closer to its reflection in salt
shallows. Deliberating,

all attention. I join in this contemplation. My intent?
To be present

on my slate perch above a shifting estuary floor.
Tide claims territory,

the heron waits. Nearby, a cormorant mocks,
dips and lifts a filmy head,

a dark pulse fracturing surface. I sigh and stretch.
Content. The sandspit

a precarious shadow, the heron unfolds, abandons
it. Unfed.

Eastward

Daylight, bauble bright, cheats year's end,
leaps and glitters on small seas of frost,
inflames the auburn banks of trees,
blue-rinses a sudden glimpse of chalk.

We swoop through modest stations, peopled
only twice a day. No one blinks.
Velocity smears hawthorn red. And I?
Concealed, a speeding shadow

in undergrowth, then a silhouette
against an emerald field.

Sun salutation

Each morning we unroll our mats
on cool grass. We are mountains,
cobras, downward-facing dogs.
The house, shuttered at our backs

stands sentry above the village
and its church, the river's lazy sweep.
This house, where once women
prayed and taught and washed

their smalls, practiced devotion,
keeping faith with life beyond
green cloistered walls. We breathe in
a taut blue canopy etched

with butterflies in flight. Breathe out
the wide, white rim of the weir.
Each morning brings its benediction:
sun catching stone.

Quarry

At first light

birds traverse this limestone desert
tip from scoured cliffs towards steel blue water
defeated in its pit.

Only the fence's tin rattle remembers the quarrymen.

Abandoning parched air the birds
launch into the green speedway of the dale
execute daily, complex performances.

A river ran here, quarrying forgiving stone.

Ran dry.

Sediment

Chasing sleep, my thoughts pursue a path across the Common
from Minchinhampton to Amberley, on to Rodborough.
Part prairie this, a tilting grassland where cattle inch
as inexorably as clouds across a spacious sky;

part playground, sedimented, hard-packed with memory.
Here's where we made our dens, proclaimed
our rules. Here's where we sped and teetered
on a turning world, mapped its hollows and raised veins

on our internal landscapes. So that, sleepless
in a grainy city light, I can still navigate to Rodborough Fort,
to sit and watch the Severn's shining blade carve out its bed
below on land as flat and foreign as another country.

Ocean

This was ours, wide, green, mysterious.
Each shore a continent and we their queens.

We ruled the paths, the fields, the outhouses,
foothills, even mountains we had never seen.

We'd send feathered sailors to travel our seaways,
fretworking weed. A heron on its nest played

our sea monster. We'd shout news, treaties, threats
across swaying depths, call truces, trade sides,

our babel drowned one summer
by a steel horse, clattering by, dashing

to unimaginable places.

Landing place

i

He's drawn to water, a farmboy
without feeling for pasture.

Lands at the harbour, a shopboy
eavesdropping on cautionary

salt-crusted tales. Watches
the winds round the Nab

wrench the cobles at anchor,
sees how men pull to shore

on a smooth. Gets his feet wet
at Whitby, on sure ground

at last. Maps freedom on
unreported oceans.

ii

Last night half in sleep I heard the boiler chatter
and creak and imagined the longhouse
had loosed its moorings, launched on the slip
and set sail for Whitby, timbers tormented
by the whip and crack of a starched wind.

iii

We argued on the cliffs at Kettle Ness. I left you
glaring at the sea as if you'd seen the answer
in its milk sheen, marched on, out of step
to lower ground, waited.

Newborn

Sunrise. Light leaks from a gunmetal sky.
Oblivious to the miracle of feet on dry land
we cross the slate cloud of Lake Manapouri at eight.

By ten the jeep has devoured Wilmott Pass
and we're on the descent to Deep Cove. Wetsuits
lie like catch on sand, our clammy new skins,

kayaks loll, gaping, deadweights,
until we haul them to water, clamber in. Newborn,
ungainly, then heartbeat feeds muscle, blade

slices silk. Now we're pioneers in a green-water
labyrinth. Two hours to Malaspina, four
to Precipice Cove, six to Crooked Arm, safe harbour.

Returning from Antarctica

I shivered in the summer heat,
feared nightfall after forty days of night
and without protective clothing, walked naked.

I'd dreamt of warmer colours,
but took fright, craved instead grey rock,
marine dark seas, burnt umber skies, sheets

of prairie white, a purer palette
reducing me and my endeavours to their proper size.
Antarctica has marked me, the scoured blue ice

seared its signature inside.

Residential

She was given a room at the top of the house
but the room seemed unready for guests.
Sucked clean of detail. Naked walls,
a narrow bed, a table, chair, cupboard,
an empty shelf. Each just itself and in between
the purity of space where things might have been.

This was not what she knew. She understood
the textured maze of home, layered chaos,
history held in bulk, chronologies of passing passions
shelved and cupboarded. She knew seeping drawers in
bedside tables, breeding grounds for books and blister packs
of pills and broken spectacles, still useful,

boxes children wouldn't take away, left luggage
for a journey not yet planned, deferred. At home
she fitted neatly into spaces others left, crammed
barely held ambition into disregarded corners.
She stared at the empty space, not knowing
how to fill it. Who for? What with? She knew

they'd never picture her, waking here
unnerved, unshaped, but breathing.

Shipwreck

We're walking to Whitby, threading north
on narrow, foot-forced paths, on cliffs redrawn
by water, weather, wind, above a shifting,
guileless sea.

Despite days like this of bright blue sun
and rippling, ditchwort-clouded grass,
I'm like the wreck at Saltwick Nab,
regularly drowned.

Ahead, the Abbey's carcass waits,
a hulk on flat and unforgiving
land. I'm emptied, like its windows,
spaced and dark.

I'm the harbour's whalebone jaw,
I'm spent. We descend for
comforts tying me to now—
tea and cake,

fish and chips. Small fry.
Out on the Nab, the salted wreck
lies broken on recycling sand, prow
pointing to the sky.

Gift

When I'm in so deep air fizzes, muffling
words and touch, when I sway on the brink

of blackness, so close to diving in, sometimes
I think of you. Silently encoded, your gift

flows thickly through my quarried veins,
inebriating as the damson gin you uncorked

and pressed on me on Sunday afternoons.
but secret, not wrapped, not labelled,

one you hoarded even though they laid you out,
wired you up, tried to steal it from you.

State of fluox

Emerging from Meadowhall to February sunshine
I catch a bodyful of benign golden arrows.

It takes days to extract each one, place it
carefully, in a gilded bowl imagined for the purpose.

Now there's a membrane containing my skinful
of misery, no more seeping, weeping, overwhelming.

Now there's something between me and despair,
new territory beneath my feet. I can't see the edges.

Easier to balance when I know I'm not going to fall.

Glee

I expected wrinkles, yes
but not skin so lacking in enthusiasm
slackening relentlessly.

Grey hairs, yes, but not sharing space
with this stranger in the glass knowing
that stranger to be me.

I expected flushes, but not the following
rush of icy cool, the flapping
and the chattering at night.

Fatigue, yes, but not such utter weariness
at man's recycling inhumanity
to man, woman, child …

You'll become invisible, they said. They
didn't say invisibility bestows liberty,
potency, secret glee!

Spacewalk

in memory of Debra Boyask with acknowledgements to Lemon Jelly

You undocked in April
stepped out into indigo in the midst of gathering green.
Your house was in order. You'd married Ms Right,
informed the authorities you wouldn't be back.
The hatch opened.
You'd gone.
Copy that.

I imagine you
filling those lungs with something more friendly than air,
navigating by light that's older than time,
marvelling at what passes for ordinary out there.
I picture you
feeling a million dollars,
light as air.

Blue

The suitcase lonely in the hall
still holds the things I grabbed when you,
surprised by pain, lay briefly on the kitchen floor,

suggested dialling nine, nine, nine, asked
if I would pack a nightdress and your book

as if this were an unexpected break
and you might sit and read beside
an azure pool or turquoise fountain ...

not take a trip bound and laced with tubes,
smiling at a distant view, fading, going blue.

Pear drops

I want to die, she said, lying in Ward Three,
still point in a tangle of technology, TV remote
out of reach. No one heard.

I want to go to sleep and not wake up
she said, imagining the pleasure
that would bring. Her daughter shook her head.

It's teatime Rose, they said.
Let's prop you up a bit. We need to make you strong.
Rose shook her head.

I want to die, she said and wondered
what she'd miss. Pear drops, she thought.
The way her daughter's frown matched his.

A twentieth century man

I'm six, secure within the salty cavern
of my father's arms. We speak
of the millennium and count
the unimaginable years …

You'll be thirty three he tells me,
I'll be sixty-eight. But

he is already ancient and all knowing.
He can pitch a tent taut, draw faces
people recognise, forecast the passing
of a storm. But this

he didn't know. That he would die
at sixty-five. A twentieth-century man.

Anniversary

We sat outside tonight
sallow indoor creatures blinking
in the teeming air

the sky already hazed,
withdrawn, a pause before
tomorrow's blue

and on the feeder, visitors
like us, two goldfinches, gleaming
and in urgent conversation.

An empty chair reminds me
of this time last year. You sat here
elegant as ever. You would

have known the details
of the birds' long flight.
You would have read the book.

You would have loved the summer light.

What living is

We were chasing the dead that day, travelling west
through lowlands of drift-deep green, edged
with cloud-water, compressed by sky;

 chasing blood-thick threads through
unremarkable towns, trying untranslatable streets
on for size. Excavating the names of the dead.

Among sodden stone records and lumpen, brown grass,
the mapping of dates on desire to belong,
your thoughts turned to somebody recently passed,

We toasted her later, you rehearsed her best moments,
how much she was missed. Then, the past drawing level,
we talked of how love can survive a cold climate

and what living is.

In the video of my sister's wedding

you play the father of the bride, clean-shaven penguin-suited
toiling up the hill. People wait outside the squat-limbed church

admiring. The procession takes its time, the eagle-eyed
will see determination in your grip as well as pride. And

at the top the camera pans to catch you, chest heaving,
chasing air. You turn aside. You make it down the aisle.

Shoulders stiff, you give her up, relieved that one of us at least
has done the decent thing and you were there to see it,

then the camera pans away… Fast forward to your speech
cheeks bright with a steroidal flush, the joker still, you play the crowd.

My mother rolls her eyes, her face a map of broken nights
and hospital appointments. You kiss her hand, you chide the groom,

you raise a toast in celebration and farewell.

Mutual acquaintance

Your eyes are shining. The *coincidence* of it!
I could have said—Beware. She will consume
you, take the nourishment you give
and spit you out. Should I have said
your admiration, in whose warmth she basks,
will turn brittle, unreciprocated? I would
have said that I was the first of many
stepping stones along her path …

but you would have thought me a sour prophet
and she would have thought so little of it.

The naming of things

Away from you, I memorise a new skyline,
annotate a leviathan anatomy,
establish myself among granite hulks
and silver ghylls. A child
reciting a times table:
Whin Rigg, Irton Pike, Lackbarrow, Scafell.

Your sentences are pitted now,
potholes sometimes, blanks
where names and places,
proper nouns should be.

We play games to fill the
spaces. Begins with?
Three guesses? We smile.
Dumb conspirators.

Can we name it? he'd said.
Can we talk in plain English
You'd nodded, half-smiling
mystified.

Travelling home

Two weeks before the longest day I turn
my back on Sheffield's gritstone and green paths,
slide into rush hour traffic, channelled south
on tarmac decked with hedgerows
and cones. After Birmingham

Cotswold limestone shoulders proud
of flood-fed fields and teeming branches.
Daylight holds its note, roads clear. I wonder
what I'll see of you and what I'll miss
and if when I arrive, your gaze will

miss a beat

       before we kiss.

Hearting

They're repairing the wall on the lane
where you live. The years have worn
the face of it, but the heart remains

true. They weigh each stone, hands
gloved in yellow dust, matchmake
angles, planes; pick, choose,

at
their feet
butter crumbs heap

and scatter, stones once intact
that slipped, shattered. Inside
our house, memories, not mine,

but borrowed from you, are slipping
too. Stories shapeshift, fragment,
childish certainties float untethered.

We'll patch up
the gaps,
the heart of things

remains

Turquoise

For the second funeral in as many weeks
she wore turquoise. The old Navy boys
looked askance.

She didn't mean disrespect. She was tired
of attending so many endings, waiting
with silver-haired friends as death

came at them, a stopping train. Turquoise
was her defence: *I'm still here.* A jewel
in the gloom, a kingfisher

flashing low in shadow. When they said
the Lord's Prayer she bowed her head,
emphasised *the glory.*

Station Piano

A workhorse, stabled between the cash machine and M&S,
past its best, not stretched by Sheffield's commuters

though regularly exercised. One man visits daily, rattles off
the classics, soupy ballads, Dancing Queen, interchangeably.

Same tempo. A guard coaxes delicacies from withered keys
before he boards the six fifteen. A student Facebooks his performance

(he's practised, surely?). Mostly men. This morning two
with filthy clothes and devastated faces, dare one another

to take turns, transgress. Every note a mystery to the novice.
A revelation. He grins—this is free? The other,

fingers stumbling, itching, reaching for a chord, finding it,
a thing of beauty, finding more, recalls a thread of memory

life
less
unravelled.

The seven eighteen

Somewhere between Derby and Leicester
sunlight scales morning's precipice
casts acid tints on speeding fields
explodes through dust-scarred windows
crowns the conductor a messiah
a looming superhero, armed and ready,
enthrones the woman opposite in red velvet
gilds her in January light. Luminous,
admiring herself in her phone.

Just After Tamworth

We're in rows, heads bowed,
enacting morning rituals,
plugged in, when someone
speaks into the cluttered quiet.

I am the Baby Jesus.
A stolid man, bareheaded,
neatly dressed, alone
speaks clearly, with conviction.

I am the Baby Jesus.
You reject me but I know
you. I am come to save
you. No comment

though eyebrows rise and eyes
are rolled. Strangers exchange
awkward smiles. He repeats
I am the Baby Jesus.

Good for you mate
someone replies, releasing
collegial smirks—and other voices
tumbling unrestrained,

a litany of pain in monotone.
My father is that way inclined.
It makes my mother sad. I never
told. I'll kill him. I am the Baby Jesus.

Smiles fade. At New Street
we collect our bags, escape.
He follows us, all of him,
jostling on the platform.

Two wheels, early,

Puncturing stillness with speed in a city behind closed doors
below a backlit September sky, clouds unwillling to commit.
Inhaling spiced air from Eid kitchens on Glen and Glover,
past Door Deals, First in Finishing, New and Re-usable Steels
on Saxon, low-slung beside the turquoise high rise of the mosque.
Swerving potholes and roadworks as yet unrelated, luxuriate
on Shoreham's silken stretch, freewheeling, exhaling...
wide curve on Clough, nippy at the lights, black cab grumbling
at my back wheel, catch the stink and the molten glow
of the tool press through open doors. Agile, navigating cabbies
deep in conversation, the man who rocks, beseeching,
at the station door ...

guilt, sweat, lock,
leave.